Yes, Yes, Yes:

The Unauthorized Biography

of

Destiny's Child .

A Tale of
Destiny, Fame, and Fortune

By Kelly Kenyatta

Busta Books
Hollywood

j 781.643
KEN

YES! YESI YES!
THE UNAUTHORIZED BIOGRAPHY OF DESTINY'S CHILD
A TALE OF DESTINY, FAME AND FORTUNE
By Kelly Kenyatta

Published by: BUSTA Books
A Division of Amber Books
1334 East Chandler Boulevard, Suite 5-D67 Phoenix, AZ 85048
e-mail: AMBERBK@aol.com

Amber Books are available at special discounts for bulk purchases, sales promotions, fundraising or educational purposes. For details, contact: Special Sales Department, Amber Books, 1334 East Chandler Boulevard, Suite 5-D67, Phoenix, AZ 86048, USA.

Library of Congress Cataloging-in Publication

Kenyatta, Kelly
    Yes, yes, yes : the unauthorized biography of Destiny's Child : a tale of destiny, fame, and fortune / by Kelly Kenyatta.
        P.cm.
    1. Destiny's Child (Musical group)--Juvenile literature. 2. Singers--United States--Biography--Juvenile literature. [1. Destiny's Child (Musical group) 2. Singers 3. Afro-Americans--Biography. 4. Women--Biography. 5. Rhythm and blues music.] I. Title.

    ML3930,D43 K4 2000
    782,421643'092'2--dc21
    [B]   00-041368

10 9 8 7 6 5 4 3

First Printing July 2000

To Andi, Harrieshia and Lil' Lizzie in memory of Spring 1998 in Ingleside, MS. Love ya, Auntie-Couz

Introduction

From the early 1990s to February 2000, Destiny's Child was comprised of four enormously talented, remarkably beautiful girls from Houston Texas: Beyoncé Knowles, Kelendria Rowland, LaTavia Roberson and LeToya Luckett. After releasing *Destiny's Child* (1998) and *The Writing's On The Wall* (1999), the girls are considered to be among the most talented new artists on the scene by industry professionals and fans.

It was predicted by some that Destiny's Child would emerge as the leading female group on the scene and the popular quartet was compared favorably to En Vogue and the Supremes.

The group swept the 1999 Soul Train Lady of Soul Awards winning three honors for its self-titled first album that went platinum. *The Writing's On The Wall* was an even bigger hit. It went double platinum within months of its release and earned Destiny's Child two Grammy Award nominations. The girls toured nationally and internationally, released hit videos, acted on television and won legions of fans around the world.

But in February of 2000, at the pinnacle of the group's success thus far, the much-loved LaTavia Roberson and LeToya Luckett separated from Destiny's Child, though continuing to pursue other dreams. Destiny's Child fans can undoubtedly expect great things from LaTavia and LeToya.

Meanwhile, the talented and attractive Farrah Franklin and Michelle Williams have joined the ever-popular Beyoncé and Kelly, keeping a quartet in place. Destiny's Child continues to shine with domestic and European tours and a hit new video. The track "Say My Name" from *The Writing's On The Wall* album has become a #1 single in the country.

Yes, Yes, Yes: The Unauthorized Biography of Destiny's Child is the story of the rise and success of the founding members who made the group an important force in the music industry. It is the story of girls who reached out and touched the lives of young people, of girls who opened their arms and accepted the love of their fans to become the #1 R&B female group in the world.

It's the story of destiny, fame, and fortune.

Yes, Yes, Yes...

Destiny's Child Original Members
Fun 4-11-11

Beyoncé

(pronounced be-on-say)
Last Name: Knowles
Age: 18
Birthday: September 4, 1981
Star Sign: Virgo
Sings: Lead Vocals

Relationships with guys

Beyoncé: . . . . No boyfriend
Kelly: . . . . No boyfriend
LaTavia: . . . . Has a boyfriend
LeToya: . . . . Working on a relationship

Where they live

Still live with parents in Houston and do
the normal things like go to the mall.

How the group got its name

Tina Knowles, Beyoncé's mom, was looking through the Bible when the girl's picture fell out. Underneath was a scripture with the word "Destiny" and they added Child.

What they love about being in show business

Traveling all over the world and meeting great people and the love and support of fans.

Goal for the group

The singers want Destiny's Child to be a household name. And they want to be great entertainers (which they already are!).

Destiny's Child put college plans on hold for now but the girls definitely plan to go. Their choices are Clark-Atlanta, Fisk, and Howard.

Kelendria

Last Name: Rowland
Age: 19
Birthday: February 11, 1981
Star Sign: Aquarius
Sings: Second Lead

The group's advice for teens today

"Be yourselves and don't fall into peer pressure. Always stay positive and stick to what you believe in. Don't always try to be a part of the crowd."

Musical roots

Beyoncé's mom sang with a group, though not professionally. LaTavia's dad, who plays instruments, was a music major in college. LeToya's dad sings and her mom is a country singer. Kelly is the first musician in her family.

Their relationship with each other

They are great friends. The girls are not blood relatives but say they feel like they sisters. It seems they're always working together but know how to give each other space. And sometimes they kick back and meditate with each other without saying a word.

Some of the many awards Destiny's Child has won

- Three Soul Train Lady of Soul Awards

- MOBO Award for Best International R &B Act

- NAACP Image Award

Do they get nervous on stage?

It depends on the crowd or the performance. The group did a new song on "Teen Summit" and was kind of nervous.

LeToya

Former Original Member
Last Name: Luckett
Age: 19
Birthday: March 11, 1981
Star Sign: Pisces
Sings: Soprano

Religion

Christians. Girls say they are "good role models, positive role models."

Advice to aspiring artists

"The most important thing is to perform as much as you can. Always give 110 percent. Stay tight with your group and find a good manager that you can trust. Keep all negativity away."

Their role models

En Vogue, Lauryn Hill, and Boys II Men

Other entertainers they like

After working with Missy Elliott, Destiny's Child says she is great. She is so funny and is the sweetest person. "We really got close to her and love her so much."

They met Monica and say she is very nice. So are the members of 702 and Blaque.

Destiny's Child also likes Lenny Kravitz and Jewel. The group loves gospel music and some favorite artists are Karen Clark and Kirk Franklin with the New Nation, and of course, all the Winans.

They still get star struck when they see certain people like Whitney Houston and Janet Jackson.

Other Interests

- Modeling and acting. Destiny's Child was written into the script of a "Smart Guy" episode on the Disney Channel.

- All four girls have appeared in sleek advertisements for Soft & Beautiful Botanicals hair products.

Yes, Yes, Yes...

LaTavia

Former Original Member
Last Name: Roberson
Age: 18
Birthday: November 1, 1981
Star Sign: Scorpio
Sings: Low Alto

Ages

Age is a subject the girls are not that keen on discussing and for obvious reasons: discrimination toward youths. LaTavia points out the focus "should be on the music, not the age." These teens wake up at 4 a.m. and go like "energized" bunnies doing the same things as artists older than they. So if you want to talk numbers, Destiny's Child would much rather talk number of hits.

15

Yes, Yes, Yes...

Cars

Beyoncé: . drives a convertible Jaguar
Kelly: . . . . drives a BMW
LaTavia and LeToya: . . . . . . no cars yet

Church

St. John's Methodist Church in Houston

Some favorite songs

Marvin Gaye's "Let's Get It On" and "What's Goin' On"

Isley Brother's "For the Love of You"

About the new members:

Farrah

Last Name: Franklin
Age: 18
Hometown: Los Angeles
Relocated to Houston
Sings: Soprano

In their spare time

They like to chill at home and talk on the phone.

LeToya is a phone junky born with a phone in her hand.

Yes, Yes, Yes…

18

Michelle

Last Name: Williams
Age: 19
Hometown: Rockford, IL
Relocated to Houston
Sings: Alto

More Fun Stuff

Here is a message from Destiny's Child to their fans:

"If we are in public and you see us, please say hi."

And the girls want you to know they read all of their fan mail and answer a lot of it themselves. If people leave their number, they will try to call them back. Of course this can be hard to do because their schedule is so demanding.

Yes, Yes, Yes...

Contents

Yes, Yes, Yes...

In the Beginning

The story of the four fabulous singers known as Destiny's Child sounds very much like a fairytale. After all, there are many of the same ingredients that make up fairytales, for example, lovely girls. From Houston, Texas, come Beyoncé Knowles, Kelendria "Kelly" Rowland, LaTavia Roberson and LeToya Luckett. The teens are blessed with such wonderful voices they have been compared to great artists like The Supremes and En Vogue. In the beauty department, and that's inside and outside, neither Cinderella nor Rapunzel has anything on these girls. And similar to fairytale life, the lives of Destiny's Child are filled with happiness and many dreams come true.

The girls might pinch themselves on occasion to see if their lives are real; they can rest assured their success is bonafide. To prove it, they've got millions of fans, fan clubs, videos, advertising contracts and two hit albums, *Destiny's Child* and *The Writing's On The Wall*.

Unlike a fairytale, the girls didn't become successful because a fairy godmother waved a magic wand. No, No, No. We are talking about "da real world," as their friend Missy Elliott might say it. Their success is a result of many years of hard work developing their God-given talents. They also have had the good fortune to be managed by Mathew Knowles, Beyoncé's father, who naturally would put the best interest of Beyoncé, Kelly, LaTavia and LeToya first.

Some people are in wonderment that the young girls have been able to break into such a competitive field and perform at the accomplished level they do. "What's their secret?" people ask. "What is it that allows them to stand out in star-studded crowds?"

Knowles told a local reporter, "There is no gimmick. The girls can really sing. They are attractive, intelligent and spiritual. They are Christians. They are humble. Their image comes from within."

With a manager who knows them so well and believes in them, how can the singers not win? But Knowles hasn't always been the manager. Let's start the story of Destiny's Child right from the beginning.

The group began as Girls Tyme in 1991 when Andretta Tillman, later Destiny's Child's co-manager and mentor, auditioned 30 girls. Six were chosen, which included all members except LeToya, who would join Beyoncé, Kelly and LaTavia over a year later.

The talented Girls Tyme, made up of 10-
and 11-years-olds, attracted a lot of atten-
tion in Houston almost immediately. The
fact that they were young and talented
was undoubtedly the key to their success,
but the girls appeared on the scene when
boy groups dominated. Perhaps the time
was ripe. There was Kriss Kross, Another
Bad Creation, New Edition, New Kids on
the Block, Hi-Five and the still popular
Boyz II Men and Jodeci. As for girl
groups, En Vogue was big and TLC was
making its mark. Undaunted, Girls Tyme
sat out to have fun while making a name
for itself. The songs they performed com-
bined R&B, rap and pop with lyrics about
boys and world unity. Sometimes spending six-hours a day rehearsing, the girls
made up most of their own dances. Their
moves were forceful and imaginative,
compelling their audiences to take notice.
Fans who remember the kids from those
days still talk about how Beyoncé, then
10 years old, pulled a little boy on stage

and serenaded him, leaving him smiling and embarrassed.

The spirited Girls Tyme built up an impressive list of appearances. It included performing at a Dallas high school where they opened for the famous Yo-Yo, and performances at the Black Expo and the Miss Black Houston Metroplex pageant. The group performed at the People's Workshop's Sammy Davis Jr. Awards, hosted by recording artist Vesta. The award was bestowed on music great Bobby Womack, who performed and gave the girls early on a taste of what their talent and dedication could bring them. They were featured on a TV magazine called "Crossroads" and the group was written about in the *Houston Chronicle*, the largest newspaper in the area. It was reported that Prince called twice asking to record them on his Paisely Park record label but that never materialized. A year after Girls Tyme formed, they made it to "Star Search," a national television show that has launched the careers of many prominent entertainers.

This was a very exciting time for the girls. They thought their singing career was about to take off, but success narrowly eluded them. After the "Star Search" appearance, important changes happened. Three of the original six members left the group and LeToya joined the remaining three girls for the quartet that became known as Destiny's Child. That also is when Knowles became manager. He was pleased with the progress of the group so far, but he determined changes were needed if the girls were to get to the next level. He took the group seriously enough to resign from his position as a neurological sales specialist. From that point, a group that would go on to leave its mark in the music industry was in place. Four young girls, though from different parts of Houston all attending different schools, were on their way to developing great friendships that would last for years to come. They would be spending so much time together they would become as close as sisters.

LeToya arrived for rehearsal from Houston's south side while LaTavia came from the northwest side and Kelly and Beyoncé from southwest Houston. Year after year, Beyoncé, Kelly, LaTavia and LeToya continued to rehearse together. They took singing and dance lessons to prepare for the great career for which they were destined. While their classmates played together after school and went to slumber parties and the mall, they missed much of that scene. They missed many a trip to AstroWorld. Instead, the girls participated in what Knowles called "Summer Camp." They kept a strict schedule where they would jog three miles each day and follow it up with eight hours of practice that included aerobics and drills.

By the time they reached high school, they had their hearts set on making it big, so they did not fall prey to the typical teen-age girl distractions, like parties and boys, even if they did sing a lot about it. They knew it would all come in time. As for the time they missed on the merry-go-rounds and swings, well, they knew the world would one-day become their playground. They were in part home-schooled, keeping rigorous schedules. Most of their time was spent with each other and with their families. In 1996, their schedules became so hectic their parents hired a tutor to help the girls with their schoolwork and to accommodate their schedules. It was very important to the girls and their parents that they got a good education while focusing on their music.

Cheryl Mitchell, LaTavia's mom, admits she was concerned with how big her destined child was dreaming. She told a local reporter she did not want to discourage her daughter, but she did want to prepare her for the possibility that "her dream might not be realized." But LaTavia said that even when it seemed their careers might not work out, she never lost hope. Through good times and through the rough ones, the girls kept working toward their dreams.

Late one summer day in1997 in a recording studio in Houston, Beyoncé, Kelly, LaTavia and LeToya were there with no recording session, publicity photo sessions or any other major engagement. The girls, dressed casually in jeans and cut-offs, chatted and giggled together. A visitor was on hand, so their manager asked them to put on a little show. Destiny's Child put on an a capella performance that stunned their guest. For the girls, it was a typical performance that came so naturally. It was the kind of performance they were used to putting on in front of church audiences since they were barely teenagers starting out together. As the visitor recalls, LaTavia's deep voice drifted in first, smooth and richer than Texas oil. Kelly and LeToya's middle-range voices sauntered in to harmonize. Beyoncé's distinctive sound streamed in and the girls harmonized. The visitor on that summer day had been a writer with a local paper. Within days, an article appeared in the paper with the writer commenting the performance was an "aural collage so beautiful it could hardly have come from the four teenagers."

The *Houston Chronicle* reporter wrote: "It was as if a quartet of angels had descended from the heavens. Don't be surprised if you see these Houston teens set the rhythm-and-blues industry on its ear in the next few months." That's exactly what they did. The girls were already on their way.

Destiny's Child, the First Album

The year leading up to the release of Destiny's Child self-titled first album in February of 1998 was undoubtedly one of the girls' most exciting years so far. They were preparing to produce the album on the Columbia record label, which meant they would be moving into music's major league. Before the album was completed, it seemed a lot of key people in the industry were taking notice of the girls and could predict their success. They were even willing to aid in it. The group was able to attract some of the most popular and talented people in R&B and hip-hop to work with them on *Destiny's Child*. Vincent Herbert, who produced hits for Brandy and Toni Braxton, handled two tracks. The Boys II Men's production team of Tim and Bob produced one track. Eleven of the tracks were produced by Dwayne Wiggins, of Tony, Toni, Tone.

Wiggins recalled first meeting the girls through a friend who signed them to a production deal when they were 10 and 11. Then in 1996, before they signed with Columbia Records, a friend played the girls' voices to him over the phone.

"I was just blown away," Wiggins told the *Houston Chronicle*. "And when they told me their ages, I was like "Yeah, right.' First of all, anyone this good would already have a deal. And no one that young would be able to blow like that."

Things were heating up for Destiny's Child. The teens were overjoyed to learn they would be working on their album with Wiggins at his studio in Oakland,

California. In the state's Bay Area, the girls rehearsed in one of the most beautiful parts of the country. Meanwhile, there was talk of them working with Wyclef Jean and Pras, from the Refugee Camp, Master P and JD. They could hardly contain their excitement. Week after week, they rehearsed and performed and wowed Wiggins with their talent and professionalism.

Wiggins told the *Houston Chronicle*, "I immediately knew that these girls were going to be huge. They were just like regular teenagers at times, you know, laughing and playing, which was refreshing to see. But they took their work very seriously."

The foursome worked constantly on their first album, which was mostly R&B and pop ballads with a few faster dance tracks.

Around this time, Wycleff Jean was still riveting from the mega success of The

Fugee's (Refugee Camp) album, *The Score*, and his own platinum debut solo album *Wyclef Jean Presents The Carnival Featuring Refugee Allstars*. During his successful career, he had found time to work with music greats like Michael Jackson, with Sublime and Simply Red. Still, he managed to add a promising Destiny's Child to his list of artists with whom to collaborate. He dropped into Houston in July of 1997 to do a remix of the song No, No, No at Houston's Digital Studios. Shortly after, the video shoot for the single began. Destiny's Child also collaborated with Jean and Pras on the track "Illusion"; JD, on "With Me Part I"; and Master P, on "With Me Part II."

Evidently, Columbia was confident in the group's first album. The record company, prior to the release of the album, put "Killing Time" on the soundtrack for the blockbuster "Men in Black," starring Will Smith. The girls were flown by Columbia to New York City to do an appearance at

Tower Records with Smith. They later arrived at a party at Planet Hollywood. Some of the people they have always admired were there and they mingled with them chatting and sharing laughs and congratulations. Huge celebrities there included Smith's actress wife, Jada Pinkett, Mary J. Blige and Sean "Puffy" Combs. The girls had their experience to thank for being able to handle their success and conduct themselves as young women of great maturity during the party.

Kelly told the *Houston Chronicle*, "We've done so many (shows) we can't keep track of all of them."

They had already shared the stage with double platinum SWV (Sisters With Voices), Immature and Dru Hill and had made many friends in the process. The girls give credit to SWV for having helped them learn the ins and outs of the music business.

Beyoncé told the *Houston Chronicle*, "They've been like big sisters to us. They've talked to us about pacing ourselves and watching out for people who could be hurtful to our careers."

It was good that Destiny's Child, though young, had had the wisdom to listen to the accomplished artists. Their knowledge of the industry and experience greatly impressed Columbia during the deal-signing stage. The record company wouldn't have to worry about how the girls would conduct themselves in interviews or whether they could handle performances and fame.

When the self-title album was released that winter, Destiny's Child was reeling from the excitement. Fans grooved to their radios and stereos and glued themselves in front of their TV sets when Destiny's Child made performances. From Houston to Jackson, Mississippi, to New York, New York, to Oklahoma City,

Destiny's Child before the breakup

Destiny's Child after the breakup

*Destiny's Child
backstage at
The Apollo*

*Tommy Hilfiger
Fashion Show:
Macy's*

Destiny's Child at the Tommy Hilfiger Fashion Show at Macy's (Herald Square, NYC)

Destiny's Child, at George's Music Room in Chicago

Destiny's Child members (l-r) Kelly, LaTavia, Beyoncé and LeToya pose for photos after their performances at Illusion's nightclub.

Destiny's Child members (l-r) LeToya, LaTavia, Kelly and Beyoncé pose for photographers at George's Music Room after their in-store appearance.

Destiny's Child are interviewed by the "Mond Squad" at V-103 radio in Chicago.

Destiny's Child members (l-r) LaTavia, Kelly, Beyoncé and LeToya happily pose for a photo after an on-air radio interview before the breakup.

LeToya, LaTavia, Kelly, and Beyoncé pose pretty during happier days.

Destiny's Child greets some of their many fans.

Destiny's Child doing one of their many interviews.

Beyoncé likes meeting her young fans in person.

Beyoncé sneak a peek at the camera while Kelendria signs autographs.

to Los Angeles, California, to cities and rural areas in other parts of the world, Destiny's Child was setting audiences on musical fire.

Beyoncé, Kelly, LaTavia and LeToya were excited about their success with the exception of one big letdown; their long-time friend and mentor Andretta Tillman passed away in 1997 from lupus. To her, they dedicated "My Time has Come."

When the girls sing "And I've come much too far, and I know what's in my heart, and I know what I feel, and this time I know it's real, my time has come," they fight back the tears. They believe Tillman is looking down smiling at them, pleased that their dreams, her dreams for them, have come true. The culmination of years of hard work together had started to pay off in a big way and they didn't care that it had not happened sooner. They say it simply must not have been time for them to make their big splash.

Beyoncé said in a Houston media interview, "I don't think we were ready... We wouldn't appreciate it as much if it had happened then. Now we know just how difficult this business can be."

The wait was well worth it. "No, No, No" went platinum shortly after its release and the album became the Number 1 hit on *Billboard's* Top Albums Chart. According to *SoundScan* in June of 1999, the debut album had sold nearly half a million copies. If the girls thought everything was going at a whirlwind pace before, their activity was picking up at the pace of a hurricane. Tours would follow and so would more in-store promotions where they met and mingled with fans and signed autographs. Destiny's Child toured the country with Boys II Men, a group they looked up to and endearingly called the members "big brothers." The girls headlined a holiday tour that following December in the UK where they performed 18 shows in 17 days. That was an amazing feat for the entertainers and the fans' response was overwhelming. They brought out the crowds in arenas in the United States and in Europe. Destiny's Child was such a hit in Europe that the girls began spending one week each month there. On both sides of the Atlantic, girls emulated their style and boys fell in love with them at first sight and first sound. And if the Destiny's Child members were tired, they never showed it. It seemed they were living on buses and laughed about their bus actually feeling like home because they were on it so much. They kept on smiling and singing their hearts out and were well received wherever they went.

To punctuate the success of Destiny's Child, the group was nominated for four coveted Soul Train Lady of Soul Awards and won in three categories. That was more nominations than were received by Janet Jackson, Erykah Badu, SWV, Mary J. Blige, Aretha Franklin or any other artist that year. The girls won for best single, best album and best new artists. The momentum would continue to build.

The Writing's On The Wall

A lot of artists would have been satis-
fied to take it easy and rest on the
laurels of their first album, but not Destiny's Child. The girls kicked their ambi-
tion up a notch and really got busy on the
album that would earn them two
Grammy nominations for 2000. The first
album had taken them two and a half
years to release. Their second would take
about two and a half months. And this
time they would have more of a creative
input. Groups oftentimes don't get that
opportunity and when they do, they
might not get credit for it. Being females
in an industry that is run mostly by males
could have presented even more of a

challenge for Destiny's Child, but instead the group got its wish. The girls got to write and produce on almost all of the tracks on their next album, *The Writing's On The Wall*, released in June of 1999. What a way to further heat up the summer for fans around the world! The single "Bills, Bills, Bills" was a hit all over the country and eventually was nominated for a Grammy as Best R&B song. The track also earned Destiny's Child a Grammy nomination for Best R&B Performance by a Duo or Group with Vocals. While "No, No, No" from their debut album peaked at No. 3 on the *Billboard* Hot 100, the group outdid itself when "Bills, Bills, Bills" jumped from number 11 to number 2 then moved into the No. 1 slot on the Pop Chart. Beyoncé, Kelly, LaTavia and LeToya were eating out at a restaurant in London that special day during the summer of 1999 when they found out "Bills, Bills, Bills" had jumped to the No. 1. Squealing and jumping with joy, they obviously made people in the restaurant very curious about what was going on.

Women of all ages snapped their fingers and sang along with "Bills, Bills, Bills", but a lot of guys hated the song and asked why the girls couldn't pay their own bills. Destiny's child got a good laugh out of those guys. They must be guilty of "perpin" like the triflin' fellas in the song, the girls sassily shot back. You see, they were not asking men to pay their bills. The song was misunderstood by some of the guys.

LeToya explained in an interview in *Sister 2 Sister* magazine the meaning of the hit that seemed to escape the fellas: "The song is about a relationship and the guy is treating the girl really well in the beginning, but then later on down the line he starts taking advantage of her. He's maxing out her credit cards, buying her gifts with her own money, just being irresponsible. And we're asking him to pay back the bills that he's run up and take responsibility for his actions. We ain't asking guys to just straight out pay our bills or anything like that. We aren't saying that you shouldn't help each other out in a relationship. But don't start taking advantage of each other."

As Beyoncé put it, when the guy is perpetrating with his girlfriend's car at the mall and going on shopping sprees at her expense, that couple is at the point where he pays back the bills or the two break up. The guys who had problems with that song might also have problems with some of the other sassy hits on *The Writing's On The Wall*. In "Bug A Boo", the girls sing about guys who act almost obsessed with girls, calling and paging them all the time and showing up in places they're not wanted. They also released the video that shows four girls in control of themselves, letting the guys know they are willing to socialize, but on their own terms, not because some bug a boo says "hey girl, I'm coming over right now. Be there."

"Say My Name" proved to be extremely popular number as well. It eventually became the number 1 hit in America on the *Billboard* Hot 100. Again, it was about the females saying "I'm too smart for the games you're running." The girls sing about a guy who appears to be cheating on the girl because he won't say her name during a phone conversation. She flat out tells him that someone must be there with him and if that's the case, they are so through. Similar to Christina Aquilera's top hit "I know What Girls Want," the "strong" songs were widely accepted by females who had had enough and by guys who knew the girls were telling the truth. See, for a lot of guys, the "triflin' brother" shoe didn't fit and neither did the "bug a boo" label so instead of dissing Destiny's Child, they respected the group and snapped the albums up as quickly as they could hit the shelves of the record stores.

Beyoncé, Kelly, LaTavia and LeToya were especially proud of their latest album effort because they further showcased their multi-talents. While being pretty obviously has countless advantages, the girls realized they had to work harder for people to look beyond their physical appearances and realize they were sheer talent through and through.

"We've always wanted people to appreciate our vocals," Kelly told *Billboard*. "We don't want people to say, 'Oh, here's another pretty girl group.'"

"I'm excited at seeing our names in the writer and producer credits," LeToya said.

Beyoncé agreed, adding that groups are more highly regarded if members are more assertive in the creative process.

The girls recalled in an interview with *Sister 2 Sister* that the time they spent making their second album flew by because they were writing and recording on a daily basis. They wrote and co-wrote most of the songs on The Writing's On The Wall. Beyoncé even got to produce on most of the tracks. It was Destiny's Child's idea to include spoken commandments of relationships at the end of each song, for example, "Thou shalt pay bills," "Thou shalt not leave me wondering" and "Thou shalt not think you got it like that."

But much the same as with the debut album, the group worked with a number of key producers. They teamed up with Missy "Misdemeanor" Elliott on "Confessing" and were back with Wiggins for "Temptation". They worked with Kevin "She'kspere Briggs (who produced "No Scrubs" for TLC) on "Bills, Bills, Bills."

It was during the making of *The Writing's On The Wall* Mathew Knowles, Columbia executives and the other higher ups involved with Destiny's Child decided it was time to take the girls to the top. Not only were major tours arranged, but the publicity campaign involved plans for more in-store appearances where thousands of fans came out and graciously received autographs. Internet sites were planned and so was an advertising campaign promoting Soft & Beautiful Botanicals hair care products on television, radio, in magazines and on outdoor billboards. Promotional CDs containing samples of the group's music were given out in salons carrying the products. The plan to elevate Destiny's Child to the upper echelons of the music world worked.

Then at the pinnacle of the group's success, the news of Destiny's Child's breakup was announced. Naturally the February 17 announcement, just days before the Grammy ceremony, caused dismay among many of the foursome's fans. Music World Management did not say why LaTavia and LeToya left the group and neither did the departing members. The management company did report that two new members, Farrah Franklin, of Los Angeles, and Michelle Williams, of Rockford, Illinois, would join Beyoncé and Kelly. The girls already knew each other and were friends. Farrah danced in the "Bills, Bills, Bills" video. Michelle met them when she was a background singer for Monica.

Yes, Yes, Yes…

64

A New Destination? No, Still Stardom

Some fans believe the writing about the break-up may already have been on the wall. There had been some talk from callers on radio stations predicting a split was imminent. Some speculated the split would be caused by an alleged discrepancy in the girls' pay. Others claimed a rift was being caused because all of the members weren't getting a chance to showcase their talent. Some other fans who claimed to have an inside on the goings on said the departing members were leaving to pursue their education and other careers.

Regardless of what was being said by fans and insiders, Destiny's Child, management and Columbia said very little for more than a month. Media reports quoted a Columbia Records spokesperson as saying LaTavia and LeToya left the group because of creative differences.

Supposedly, it had been planned that on Grammy night, the original girls would go on stage if the group won an award. That was how fans would want it. After all, hadn't Beyoncé, Kelly, LaTavia and LeToya formed a friendship over the years that was stronger than many sisters. Importantly, the original girls had produced the hits and it was only fair they should receive the award. But the popular and longstanding TLC won in the categories where Destiny's Child had been nominated so there was little news surrounding the group at the awards. After that, the new Destiny's Child would appear together professionally. The new girls practiced more than six-hours each day and appeared in the "Say My Name" video and on the Tonight Show. Apparently the hard work paid off. The video became one of the most popular videos on television and the crowd responded positively to a fabulous performance on "The Tonight Show with Jay Leno."

Two weeks after the group restructured, the new Destiny's Child appeared on Houston's The Box radio station. Host Shelley Wade raised the topic of the break-up and asked the members to shed light on the issue and possibly dispel rumors. Wade even pointed out to Beyoncé that some people were putting the blame on her because her dad was their manager.

Beyoncé responded that such talk was upsetting. She said, "My father has done so much for everybody. As far as people saying that the reason I was lead singer was because my father was the manager, that is also totally and entirely untrue.

The lead singing is based on ability. My father has nothing to do with the decisions being made on who leads the songs. That's all up to the producer. And it's up to the artist, individually, if you want to work on yourself and better yourself so you're able to lead the songs."

She added that her father never went to the producers and asked them to let her sing. She said that actually the only time he had done that was to ask whether the other girls could sing lead.

As to why her friends left Destiny's Child, she said, "It just happened like it happened. But it doesn't have anything to do with Mathew being my father. None of that."

Wade said she knew "there were a lot of legal issues going on" that the group could not talk about but offered members a chance to further address the situation

68

if they could. Beyoncé declined saying any further talk was counterproductive.

"We're trying to work on the future and we're excited about the new girls," she said. "We're just happy because the fans are still supporting us. And the album sales are skyrocketing. We're still in the top 20 for like 28 weeks. We've been selling like 76,000 a week."

By any other public accounts, Beyoncé and Kelly wished LaTavia and LeToya well. As for the new Destiny's Child, some fans announced disappointment on Internet Web sites, letters to MTV.com and on radio stations. Others said they could accept the new girls. Regardless of what they said, fans continued to buy *The Writing's On The Wall*. Destiny's Child embarked on a European tour and on March 12 played its first live concert since Farrah and Michelle became members. The group headlined at a packed arena only days after "Say My Name" soared to

No. 1 on the *Billboard* Hot 100. Beyoncé announced on stage that worldwide sales stood at 3.5 million copies.

After completing the European tour, Destiny's Child returned to the U.S. to appear with Brian McKnight at New York's Madison Square Garden. Also on the agenda were appearances on MTV, a show in Atlantic City, N.J. and at a show at Disney World in Orlando, Florida.

Although the girls were soaring in many respects, they undoubtedly were experiencing some of their roughest times as well. Farrah and Michelle were under pressure to fill LaTavia and LeToya's platforms. Beyoncé, Kelly and the two new members had to prove to fans that the new Destiny's Child was just as much a crowd pleaser as the original cast.

LaTavia and LeToya broke their silence a month after the announcement of the new members. They said it has been falsely announced they left Destiny's Child over "creative differences." In a lawsuit they filed against manager Mathew Knowles and the members of Destiny's Child, they noted they "have not withdrawn from Destiny's Child despite defendant's wrongful and malicious efforts to force them to do so." LaTavia and LeToya claimed breach of partnership duties and breach of fiduciary duties. The suit charges that Knowles and the other singers took LaTavia and LeToya's money and kicked them out of the group. The girls charged that Knowles made money from them while they themselves made virtually no money. Gerald Conley, LaTavia and LeToya's attorney, told the *Houston Chronicle* the girls earned less than $100,000, which is much less than what multi-platinum artists should earn. Conley said his clients have had no access to Destiny's Child's financial records and that it is unclear how much money is at stake.

LaTavia and LeToya charged that Mathew Knowles, Beyoncé, and Kelly "went on a rampage to destroy (their) careers." They said they were not informed about performances including the Grammy Awards and the Soul Train Music Awards. The former members named new members Farrah and Michelle as members. The new girls appear in the *Say My Name* video "even though they had nothing whatsoever to do with it," the suit charges.

Mathew Knowles responded saying he looks forward to the day when the real truth comes out. "There are and have been many creative differences," he told MTV News.

He answered one key charge saying that there had been no misappropriation of funds. He also pointed out that LeToya and LaTavia, decided to fire, him, the manager of Destiny's Child without discussing it with the other members, Beyoncé and Kelly, which was "pretty insulting." Knowles said he was disappointed that at the highlight of their careers, LaTavia and LeToya "made a bad business decision."

It will be a while before the truth is known about why Destiny's Child split up, but the lawsuit brought an end to the speculation over why the two members actually would leave the group when it was the most successful it had ever been.

Regardless of what happens from here, the girls are faced with the goal of re-building their careers and undoubtedly mending friendships and wounds. But this is likely where all the girls' true star quality will shine through.

Merriam-Webster has numerous meanings for the word "star." The dictionary says a star is a natural luminous body visible in the sky at night. Its size may be as small as the earth or larger than the earth's orbit. A star is an outstandingly

talented performer, someone of out-
standing excellence. There are so many
ways the word can be used. And there are
millions of fans who would use it to
describe Beyoncé, Kelly, LaTavia, LeToya.
Michelle and Farrah are gaining fans, too.
The original members have proven they
can stand out in the music world, a world
of talent and glamour made up of the best
of the best. Some believe this is just the
beginning for the old and new members
of Destiny's Child. As luminous as they
are, the young women have yet to shine
their brightest.

John Moran, who owned Digital Studios
where the girls recorded three of the
tracks for their first album, billed them as
potentially the biggest act from Houston
since Clint Black.

Demette Guidry, Columbia senior VP of
black music told *Billboard* in June of 1999,
that while a lot of female groups come
and go, Columbia wants to stress that

Destiny's Child comprises girls that are songwriters and producers.

"On the first album, they were finding direction," Guidry said, adding that the second time around, the girls knew how to give their fans what they want. "We're going to continue to establish Destiny's Child as the No. 1 female group in the world," he said about the group before members changed.

Still, many good things are expected of Destiny's Child as the group prepares to release a third album. Beyoncé is expected to release a solo album with two songs written by The Artist Formerly Known as Prince. Kelly is planning to release a single "We Oughta Separate" with new artist Avant. LaTavia and LeToya are reported to be appearing in Jagged Edges's new video. Some insiders say the two girls are starting a group with a third talented girlfriend.

Remember "Cinderella" and "Beauty and the Beast?" None of the happiness happened without some hardship. In the end, the girls hopefully can all enjoy the success of Destiny's Child first two hit albums. Regardless of temporary setbacks, hey have a nearly lifelong friendship they've already established, great fans and new and exciting projects. Things are looking up for these wonderful young ladies!

More Fun Facts About Destiny's Child

Taking it Personally

(How the girls see each other. In an interview with *Sister 2 Sister*)

How the girls describe Kelly

She is the nicest person, sensitive, generous (even gives silver bangles to fans). Beyoncé describes Kelly as the type of person who would give you her sweater if you were cold, even if she's cold herself.

How the girls describe Beyoncé

She is sweet and very caring, very understanding. The other girls agree that Beyoncé reminds them of the nice aunt or the mom. Kelly said Beyoncé tells the other girls things they really need to hear.

How the girls describe LaTavia

She's real understanding and sweet. She is logical and thinks things through. LaTavia made straight A's all through school LeToya announced proudly after teasing her about being a nerd.

How the girls describe LeToya

She can make anyone laugh, even if you're in the worst mood ever. She is a good listener, non-judgmental and very forgiving. LaTavia says LeToya will listen without giving you advice and the girls agree that sometimes you need that. You just need someone to tell things to just to get them off your chest.

How Mathew Knowles sees the girls

In addition to being very talented and dedicated young ladies, Knowles says: LeToya is the fun one. She tells jokes. Kelly is intense and serious. LaTavia is sassy and although she is the youngest, she comes across as mature. Beyoncé knows exactly where she wants to go.

The Look

According to the girls, their look is not something someone sat down and decided it would be. Mainly it stemmed from the girls' individual personalities.

Kelly told *Sister 2 Sister*, "We look for stuff to fit us and our personalities and I think that's why we have such a great stylist

Tina Knowles, Beyoncé's mom. She's our personal stylist and she gets all our clothes to fit our personalities. All of our clothes are different because we get all of our clothes made. It's kinda hard to go into a store and find clothes for four different girls. We like to dress different."

For performances, their closets are stuffed with leather, Spandex, mini-skirts and crop tops that flatter their enviable figures. When the *Sister 2 Sister* journalist pointed out that "a lot of people think you're dressing too grown for your age," Kelly offered to set the record straight to anyone who thinks the girls dress too sexy: "I want you to go and look at every other teenage magazine, to a high school, to a concert and you'll see that most of those girls dress like Destiny's Child with their stomachs out and their legs out. So I don't know why we keep getting picked out of everybody else."

LeToya says she thinks the girls dress well, somewhere in the middle of not nerdy and not too sexy: "I think someone is always gonna have something to say. I guess that's the only thing they can say about us" she added.

The girls declare that when they're not performing, they're just your regular girls next door. They dress way down in jeans and t-shirts.

By the way, Destiny's Child fans give the gang a thumbs up on their off-the-hook wardrobe. When responding to a survey on a popular fan site (Jon Blaze Destiny's Child site), 89 percent of respondents said the girl's clothes are "all good."

The Mane Thang

The girls are lucky because their hair stylist is also Tina Knowles. Tina has known the girls since they were very young so she knows their personalities well. That makes it easy for her to help them get their individual glamorous and casual styles and colors.

The girls wear a wide variety of styles designed with their own hair, no exten- sions, no hair pieces (well, except when Beyoncé wore extensions once for a tour). The girls sometimes wear their hair in ponytails, braids or sleek and straight. At other times they sport shiny bouncing curls and in Kelly's case, short and chic curls. She has worn a blue-black shade for a long time. Beyoncé has worn a full head or long gorgeous braids or just two fash- ionable plaits. She often wears blonde highlights over an ash brown shade. LeToya loves short bangs in the front with the rest of her hair hanging below her shoulders. LeToya's hair is brown with golden highlights. LaTavia likes to wear her long hair swept up in the front and hanging long in the back or swept to the sides and hanging long in the back. Tina says she highlighted LaTavia's hair very light in the front and then used copper, bright red and copper to give her different tones.

Tina avoids blow-drying as much as possible because she knows the heat is hard on black hair. After she shampoos and conditions the girls' hair, she sets the hair on rollers and styles it with a flat iron after it dries.

To keep the girls' hair looking fresh and healthy, Tina gives them a deep conditioner weekly. She trims their hair every six weeks.

"The keys to keeping the hair looking beautiful are deep conditioning and trims," she told *Sophisticate's Black Hair* magazine.

On fame

Beyoncé

Fame: "As a group we've sometimes been compared to En Vogue or the young Supremes when we first came out. These are groups we've really looked up to and when people compare Destiny's Child to them, that's a compliment."

Kelly

Fame: "I didn't miss prom this year because I went with a friend! And I think that's what I really miss: the social part of school. With a career like ours, having a boyfriend is really hard because sometimes guys don't really understand your schedule. You have to have a huge amount of trust; you have to trust that person and just know that they won't hurt you."

LaTavia

Fame: "I have a boyfriend and its kind of hard to maintain a relationship because of the distance. That's why it's important to build up trust and try not to do anything to jeopardize that-because once you do, then it's very hard to gain it back."

LeToya

Fame: "It's fun being recognized by fans. But when you're in show business you always have to be smiling and have a positive attitude even though your day might be going badly. You can't have a negative attitude, because if you do that to the wrong people, then it can ruin your career. But for the most part, the people we meet don't treat us like 'superstars.' They treat us like home girls! I sign autographs, and I try to treat everybody like I want to be treated."

Source: On music and fame from Destiny's Child Official Web site

Yes, Yes, Yes…

86

The Official Destiny's Child Fan Club

www.dc-unplugged.com

Mail:
Music World Entertainment Inc.
P.O. Box 710450
Houston, TX, USA 77271-0450

Fax: 713-772-3034
Email: mwe@.swbell.net
mthomas@moyo.com

To: The fans of Destiny's Child

From: The girls
(as posted on their Web site)

"We would like to extend our thanks and invite you to our fresher than fresh fan club. This is the spot where you can get the latest, most exclusive news about us, the new album, our travels, and many more cool surprises. In addition, as members, you will receive the number to our new fanline, an e-mail newsletter, and special invitations to events in your area. We will be keeping track of each and every one of you and will periodically choose many of your e-mails and letters to personally answer. We really do appreciate all of your support and thoughts and would love for you to contribute ideas as to how we can make our fan club and dc-unplugged better. After all, this is for all of you the fans. Once again, thanks for everything."

About the Author

Kelly Kenyatta is a Chicago-based writer and freelance journalist. She has written for major newspapers and magazines and holds bachelor's and masters's degrees in journalism.

Photo Credits
Front and Back Cover: Walik Gorshon
Interior: Walik Gorshon (pgs 39-41)
Raymond Boyd (pgs. 42-48)
Mark Scott (pgs. 49-51)

Yes, Yes, Yes...

ORDER FORM

BUSTA BOOKS

Fax Orders: 480-283-0991   Telephone Orders: 480-460-1660
Postal Orders: Send Checks & Money Orders to: Busta Books
Online Orders: E-mail: bustabk@aol.com
1334 E. Chandler Blvd., Suite 5-D67, Phoenix, AZ 85048

Please send _____ copy/ies of *Yes, Yes, Yes: The Unauthorized Biography of Destiny's Child*

Name:_____

Company Name:_____

Address:_____

_____

City:_____State:____Zip:_____

Telephone: (_____) _____

E-mail:_____

For Bulk Rates Call: **480-460-1660**

Yes, Yes, Yes:The Unauthorized Biography of Destiny's Child $4.95

❑ Check ❑ Money Order ❑ Cashiers Check
❑ Credit Card:
    ❑ MC ❑ Visa ❑ Amex ❑ Discover
CC#_____ Expiration Date:_____

Payable to:
    Busta Books
    1334 E. Chandler Blvd., Suite 5-D67
    Phoenix, AZ 85048

Shipping: $3.00 per book. Allow 7 days for delivery.
Sales Tax: Add 7.05% to books shipped to AZ addresses.

Total enclosed: $_____